Spool

Spool

Andrew Brenza

SPOOL

Published by Unsolicited Press
Printed in the United States of America.
First Edition.

For information contact:
Unsolicited Press
Portland, Oregon
www.unsolicitedpress.com
orders@unsolicitedpress.com
619-354-8005

Cover Design: Kathryn Gerhardt
Editor: Jay Kristensen Jr.

ISBN: 978-1-950730-61-2

catbird/everything you see

I speak your scars
like I speak of trees
like trees speak a name
the one we live in
drupelet of sorrow
that is you, wet with song

sun series

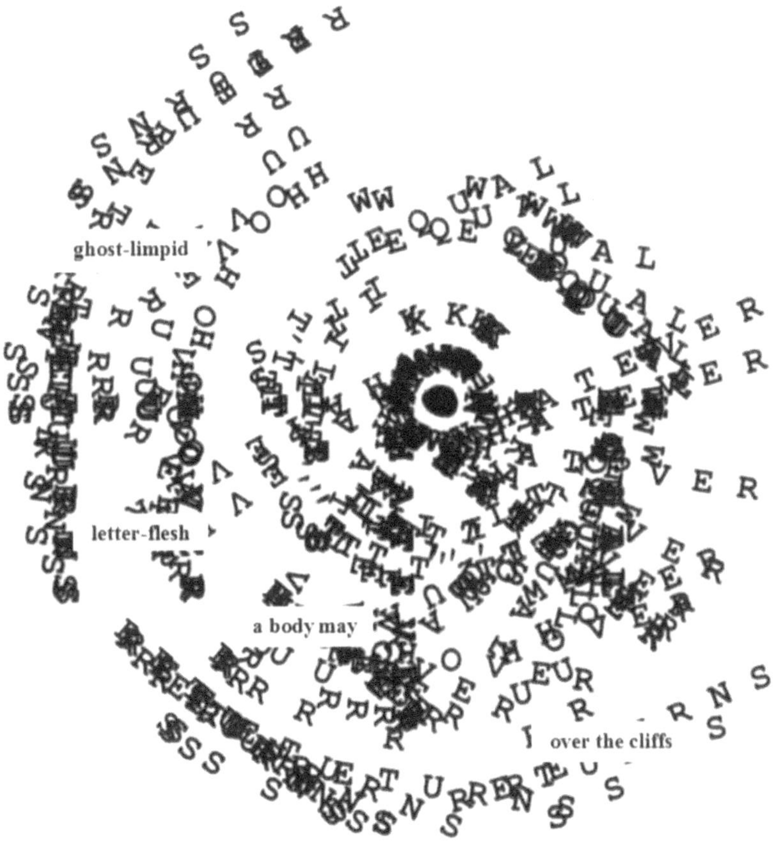

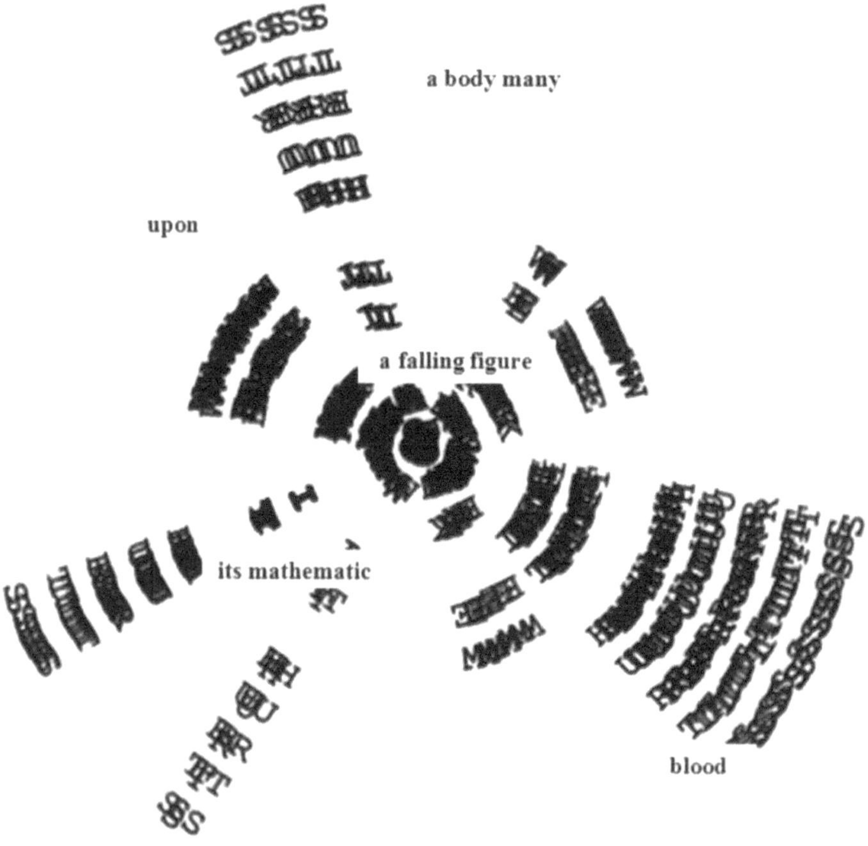
a body many
upon
a falling figure
its mathematic
blood

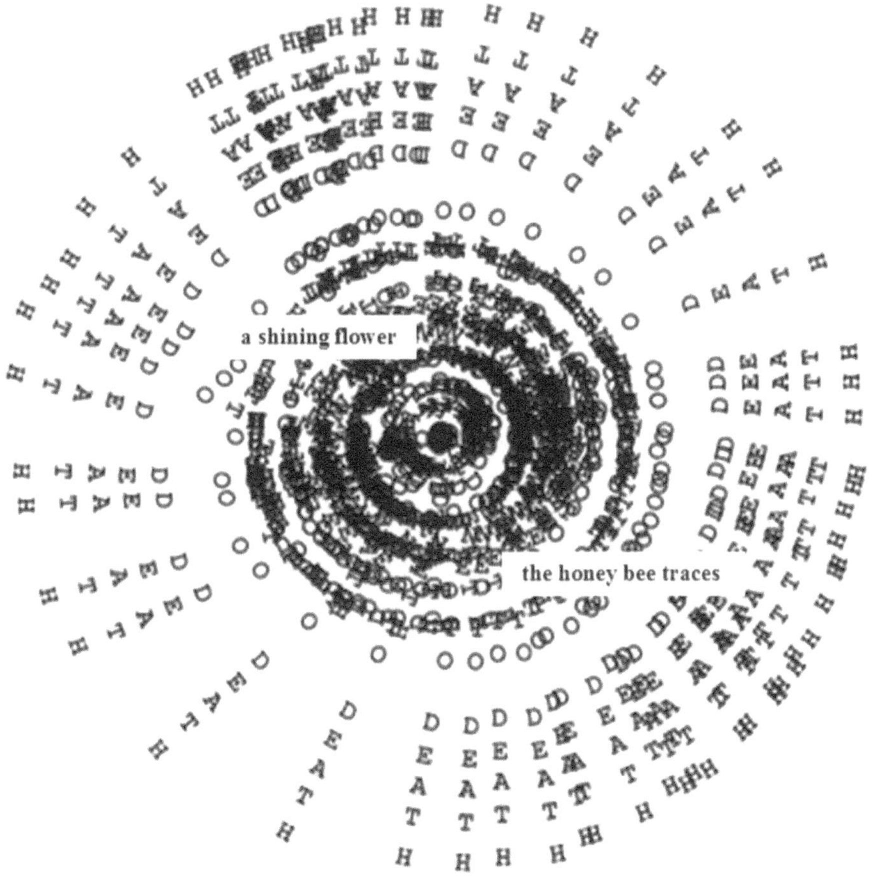
a shining flower
the honey bee traces

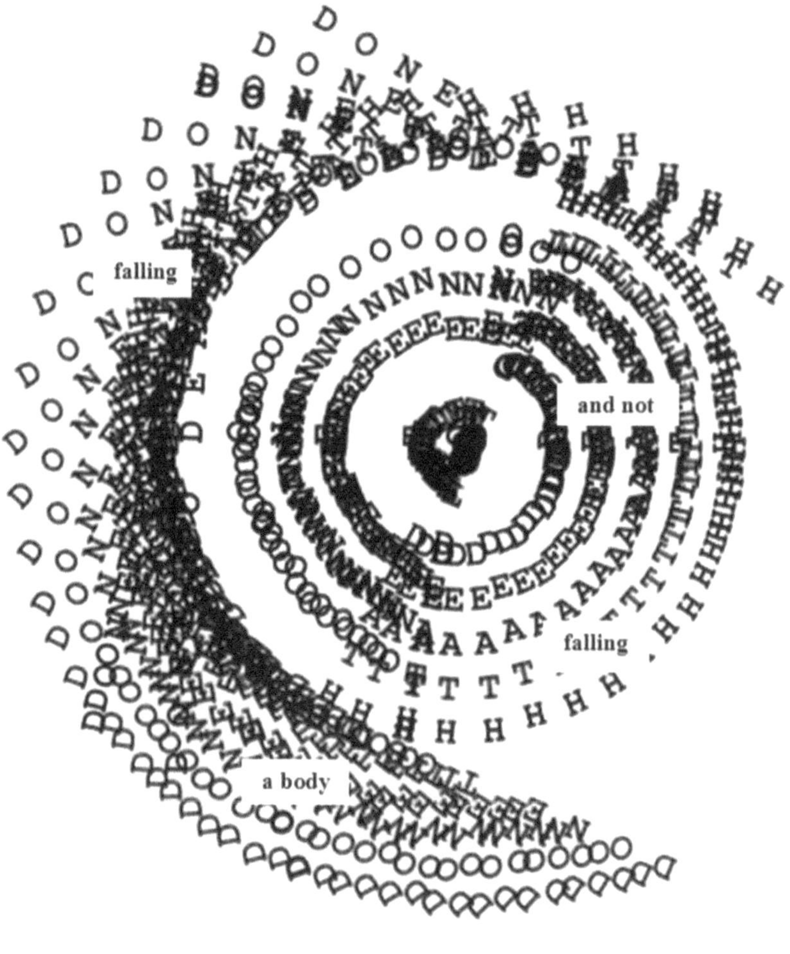
falling
and not
falling
a body

mathematical
over the cliffs
in the wind

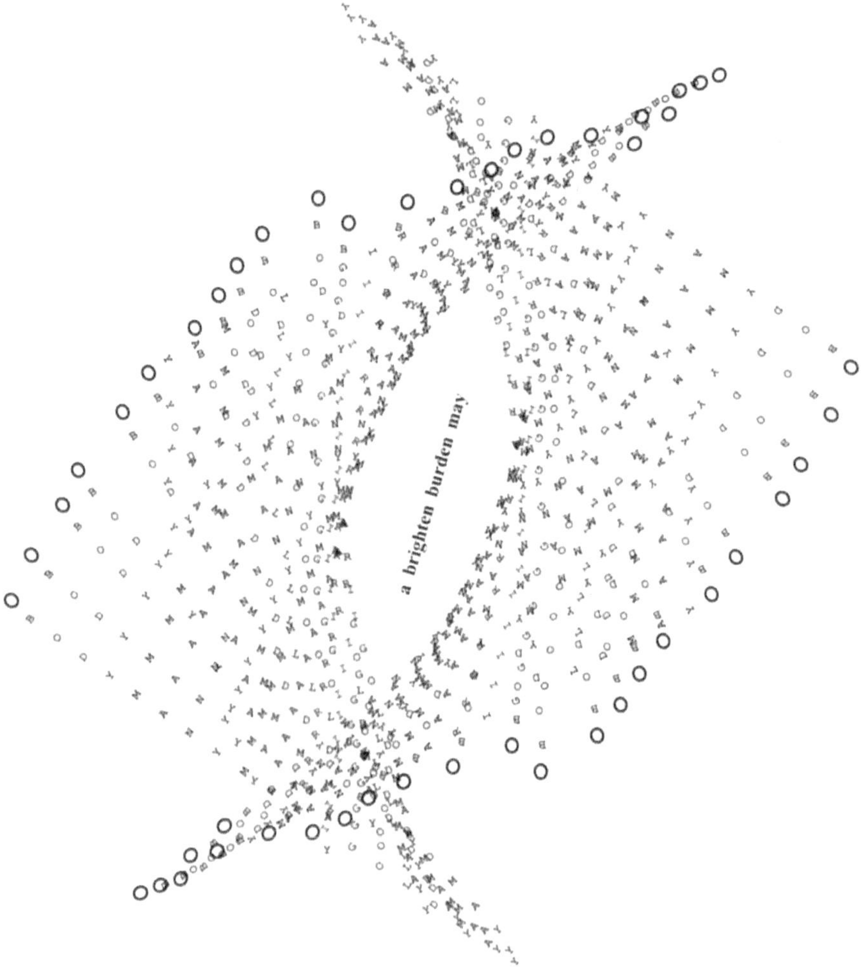
a brighten burden may

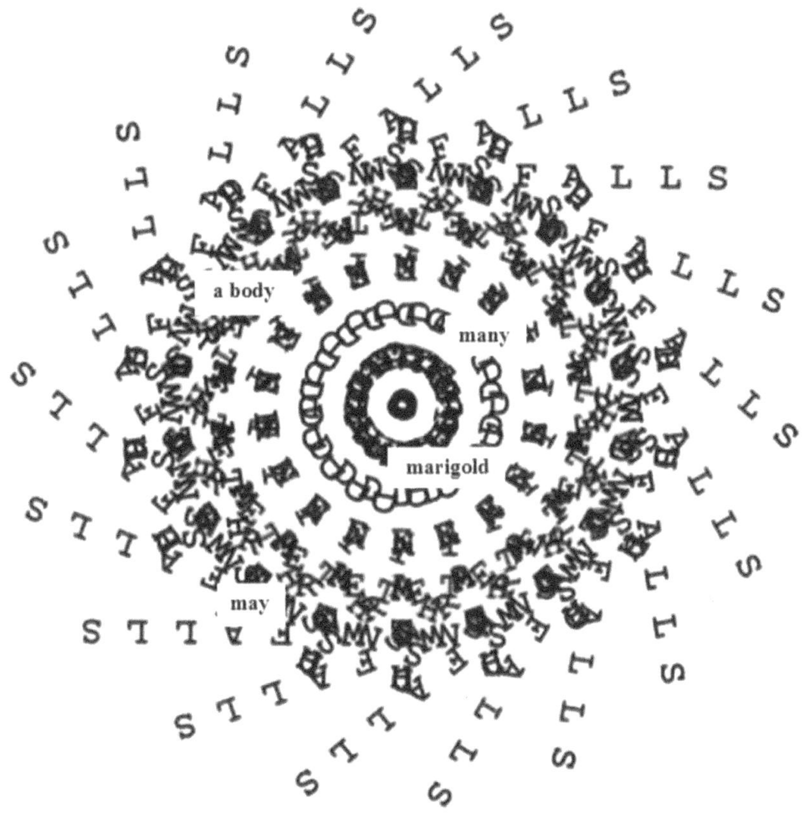
a body
many
marigold
may

road/trip

a lovely movement this
deer is an electric blank
of eyes in heart's nest
arterial tree like it's a high
way to think the body
into a vase of words
in a room we never get to

bay/scene

lift and pour
schematic
rose-empty-
facet it's every
scene like that
discomforts
in nothingness
when bay speaks its-
self in substance
to smell the shit
you cannot eat
its crabs you cannot
eat or any-
thing b/c
it just
does-
n't
car-
e   a bite
a-
bout
whatever
breath-bird
fledges in your heart today

horizon/no horizon

there is no horizon we live in
the horizon it is our skin pretending time is something
sensing wind slants, sunlight

a part/apart

this is not the shape of flame a body means
never to be alone darkness rustles rut-less soft-
petalled a conscious hum reflection's electric
company a part/apart at the same time
somehow fields of blank flowers it's unspeakable name

a concrete forest

O blooming earth

O blossom eye

O body-flowered-braid-

and-weaver-blurred light

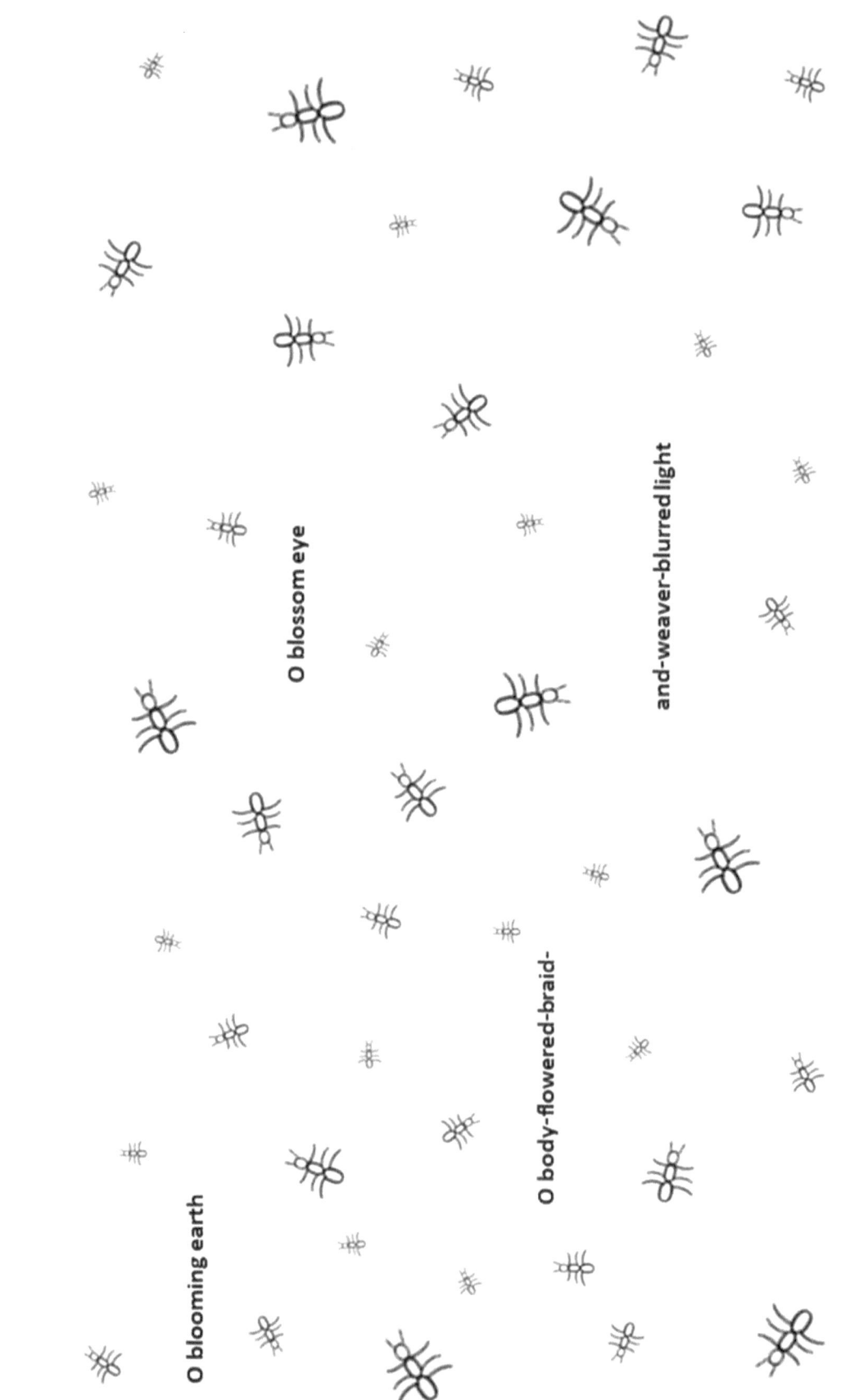

reed	reed	reed	reed
reed	reed	reed	reed
reed	reed	reed	reed
reed	reed	reed	deer
reed	reed	reed	reed

reed	reed	reed	reed
reed	reed	reed	reed
reed	reed	deer	reed
reed	reed	reed	deer
reed	reed	reed	reed

reed	reed	reed	reed
reed	reed	reed	deer
reed	reed	reed	reed
reed	reed	reed	reed
reed	reed	deer	reed

reed	reed	reed	reed
reed	reed	reed	reed
reed	reed	reed	reed
reed	reed	reed	reed
reed	reed	reed	reed

M A R Y E L L E N S O L T

MARYELLENSOLTMARYELLENSOLTMARYELLENSOLT

M A R Y E L L E N S O L T

I want to say in dusk but it is memory

and I want to say its beauty despite myself in memory

so I can say it is beauty that will continue

o filigree of fields behold me to your words

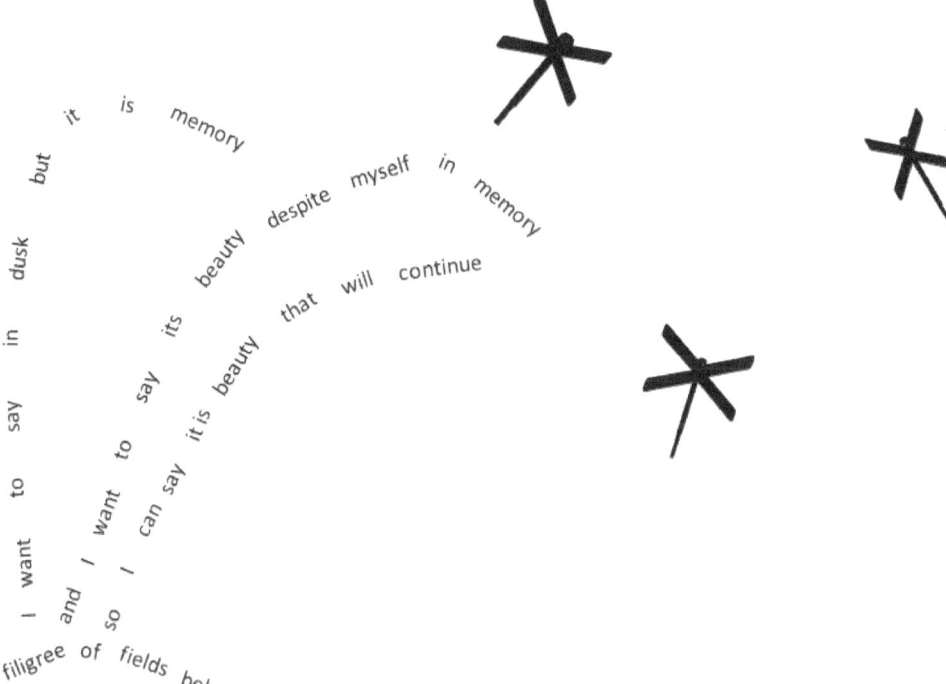

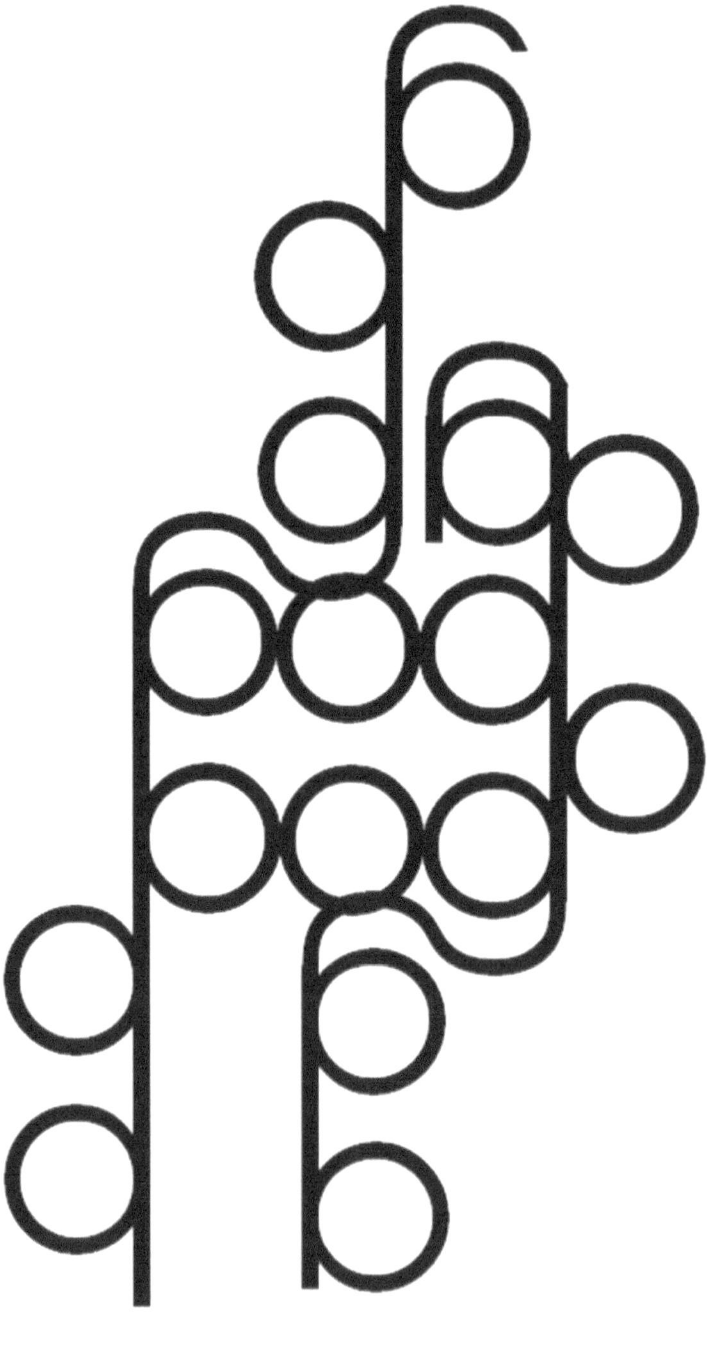

everything is around you and it is everywhere you equal to its vastness

small as a leaf fallen from its tree you totter

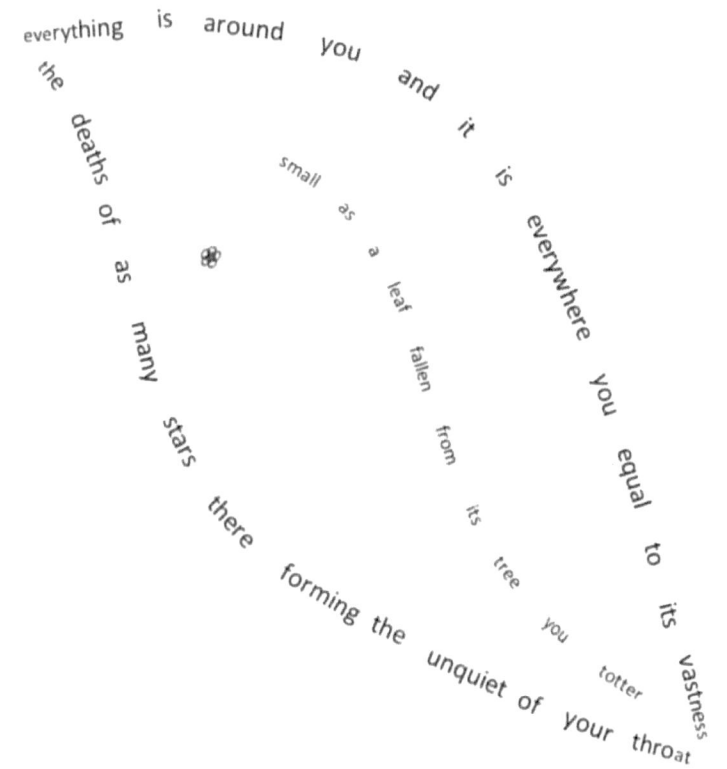

the deaths of as many stars there forming the unquiet of your throat

softly like sleep the sound and the leaves

are murmuring

so gently over the water

so come-
hither evening

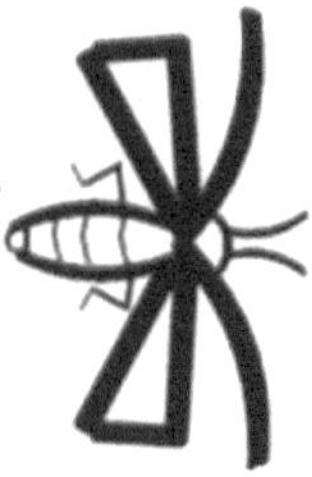

so lovely

eyes

the wisps
of light at field's

blue end

wings

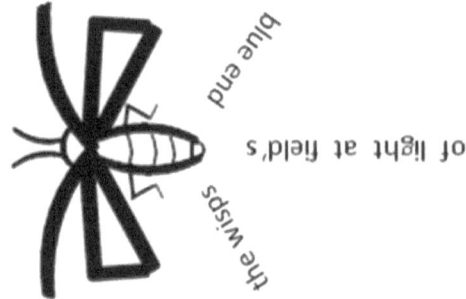

enough
to fall into

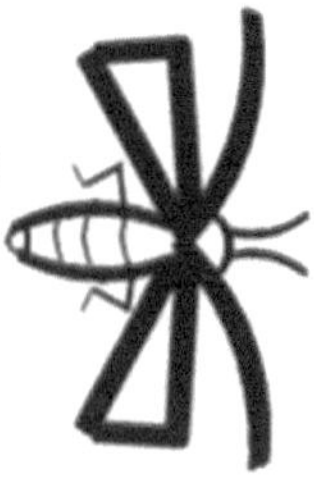

forever

commute/compute

a frigate's spiral ascension into...
call it work call it shaken call it please
and oh god who cares
all that half-brain asleep between

wulst and worsted signals
it's day down here;
to be asleep and flying
sometimes for years

it means that it means
call it shirk call it waken call it whatever oh god please

flowers/page

on pin-tip, a ragged phrase-
laced fragrant ghost-wild thing
in every sense between us

rounded/plain

lichen
on bollard
to planet
plant it
face up
little worlds
whatever
strange
stranger makes
of it yours
a body
round as
plain

eels/moths

your body
is eels'
elastics
in dance-
water
and eels'
umbral
trace

or flits
an osmic
maw-
blossom
in the dark-
ness of
your torso

blood all
historic
moths
in its gullet

bluebirds/abattoir

whatever bluebirds weep
from your bosom, 'tis but
a scratch in the attic crawl
space storage room abattoir
of indelible ruin horror
movie scrawl in which you
dribble your emptinesses
like a symbolically stuck pig
for everyone to see

knead/need

bituminous light
in hellstrip

throat-raw
fig-scratch

branch
of latex tears

in a bag
in your head

you carry
them some-

where, any-
where, your-

selves you
call

them, but not
here, never

call them
here

poem titled II

vergent snow
and so many
unconditional
stars that it is no
place but ghost-
herd to think I'm
faking this my
shadow art on
a wave of harrow
so a bull it's sleeping
I imagine by a vineyard
in Spanish grain
though lightning dims
its fringe of flowers
is it cosmos you
wonder is it strain

weed eater/flay

string become blade   thresher
bed of mint   wracked-raw
burst   a fragrant
moment   movement   the air is full
of submission   frightened by

blue lobsters/your eyes

I dream of blue lobsters as in
I am looking in your eyes

somewhere space is silhouetting
your body I want it

to be a gentleness
your breath giving shape

around you yours your hands
in whatever movement

quiet clouds of jellyfish
pulse the silences of your proliferations therein

oil/song

in-hollow
the bones of birds
weekends free
slick the oil stains
a song somewhere

tear or/terror

over the lawns of the moisturized neighborhood

T e
Ar

o r

T
E
aR

w
A
t
E r

D
r
O
P

s
W
e
A
t

s w

E e

t

B e

a

d

O

R

T e a

R

waterlight

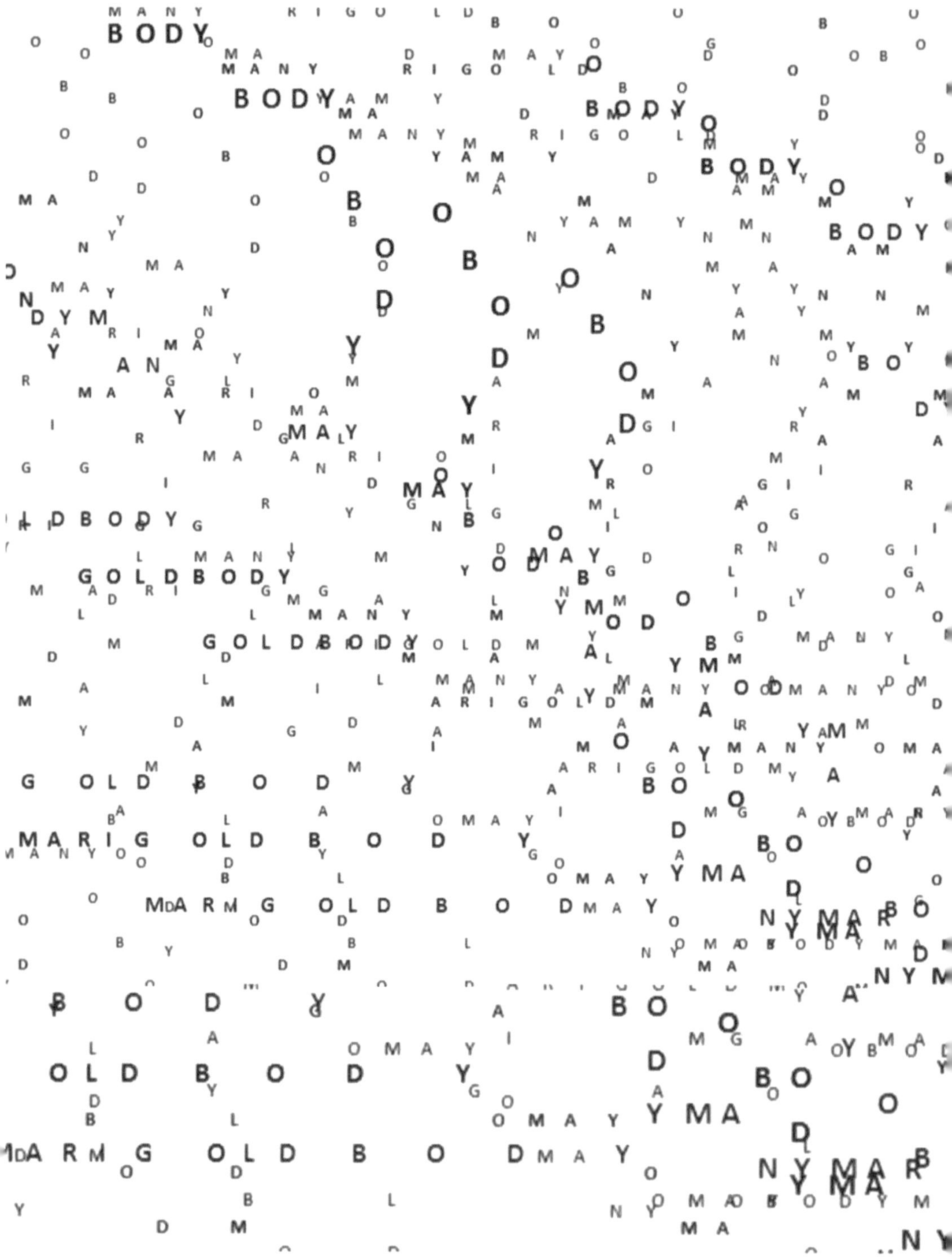
BODY
GOLDBODY
MANY
MAY

quely flashes particulate

into being so

no song sounds good forever

O G O

B O B

N Y R I G O L D O G O O O

BODY D M A Y O O D O B

M A M A M Y R I G O L D BODY D O

O O O MO A M D M M Y O YO D G O B

B B BODY M Y A BODY B O D

O O B M A N Y R I G O L D

O O N M N N M Y

D D O M A D A M A Y O

D B Y A Y Y

Y Y Y B Y A M Y B O

Y O Y M A M O N M M N N

B O O M A O M

G M A M A D A Y A Y Y

DYM N A B

A A D R I M A Y O R Y G I M R M M

A N Y Y N

R N G L O I M O A O A A

Y M A Y

Y I Y D G M A Y L R G D I R

M A A R I O M

M A Y M O D O D I Y o I

R L Y G L M A G

O L D B O D Y A Y M B G L

N Y

A R M A G O L D M M A O D M A Y D R O

M A R I G G N I

D A M A Y M A N Y Y M M A N Y O O L

G O L D B O D Y L D M A A B G D L

B O D Y G A M A B O M A

L A O M A Y I M G A O Y B M A R

O L D B O D Y B O Y

D Y G O A O O

B L O M A Y Y M A D O

R M G O L D B O D M A Y N Y M A R B O

O D O Y M A

B L N O M A B O D Y M A D

D M M A N Y M

when we needed

wholly

or unholy

a landscape

upon us

light as iridescence on a throat of feathers
our eyes straining to listen

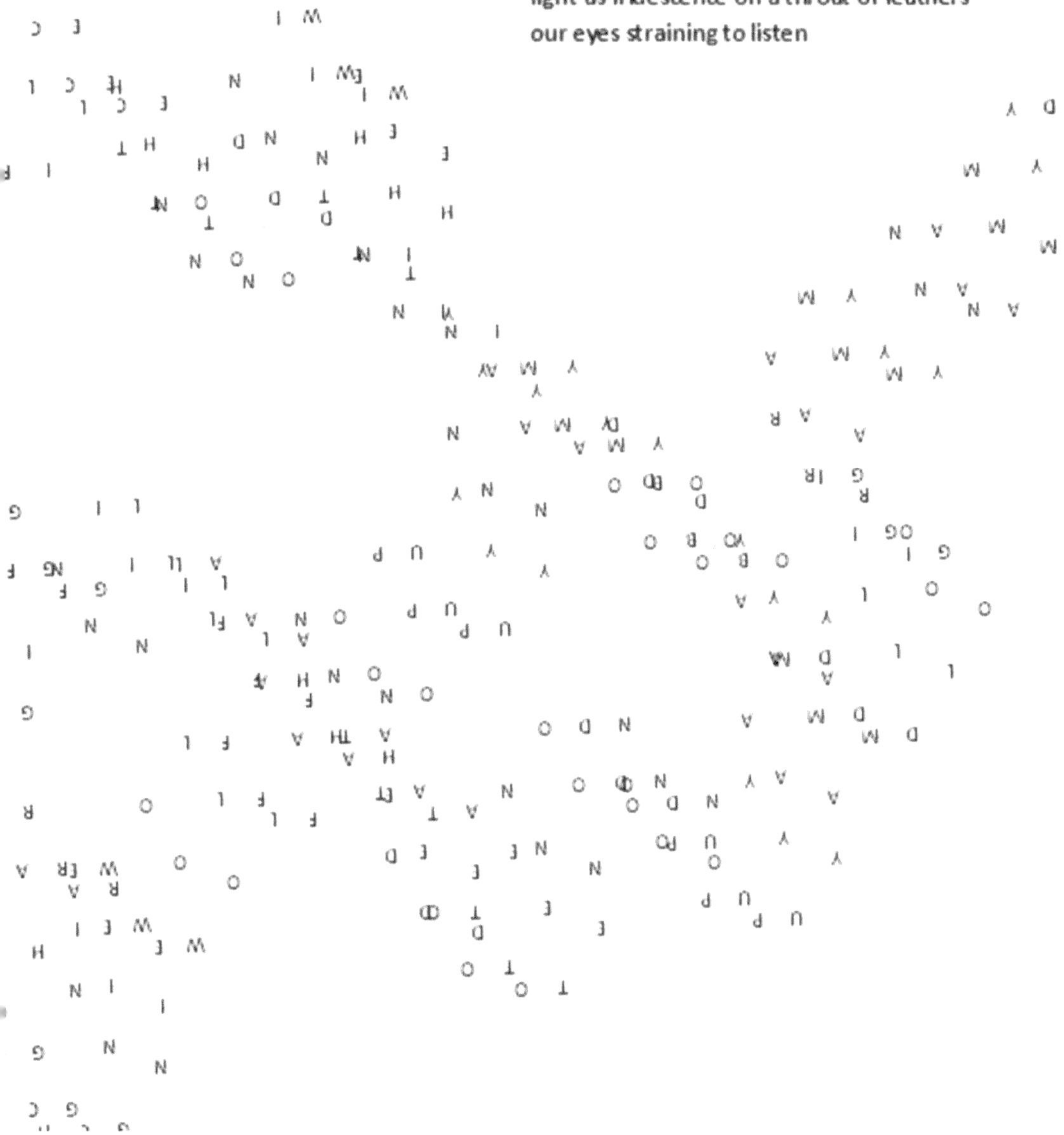

falling off trees

more human than we wanted

the sound of the sea in a bell because staring

not ghost but nothingness   machines humming air ducts planes
grass lapping at our feet a robotic nerve
I could die here   infinitely   in the way

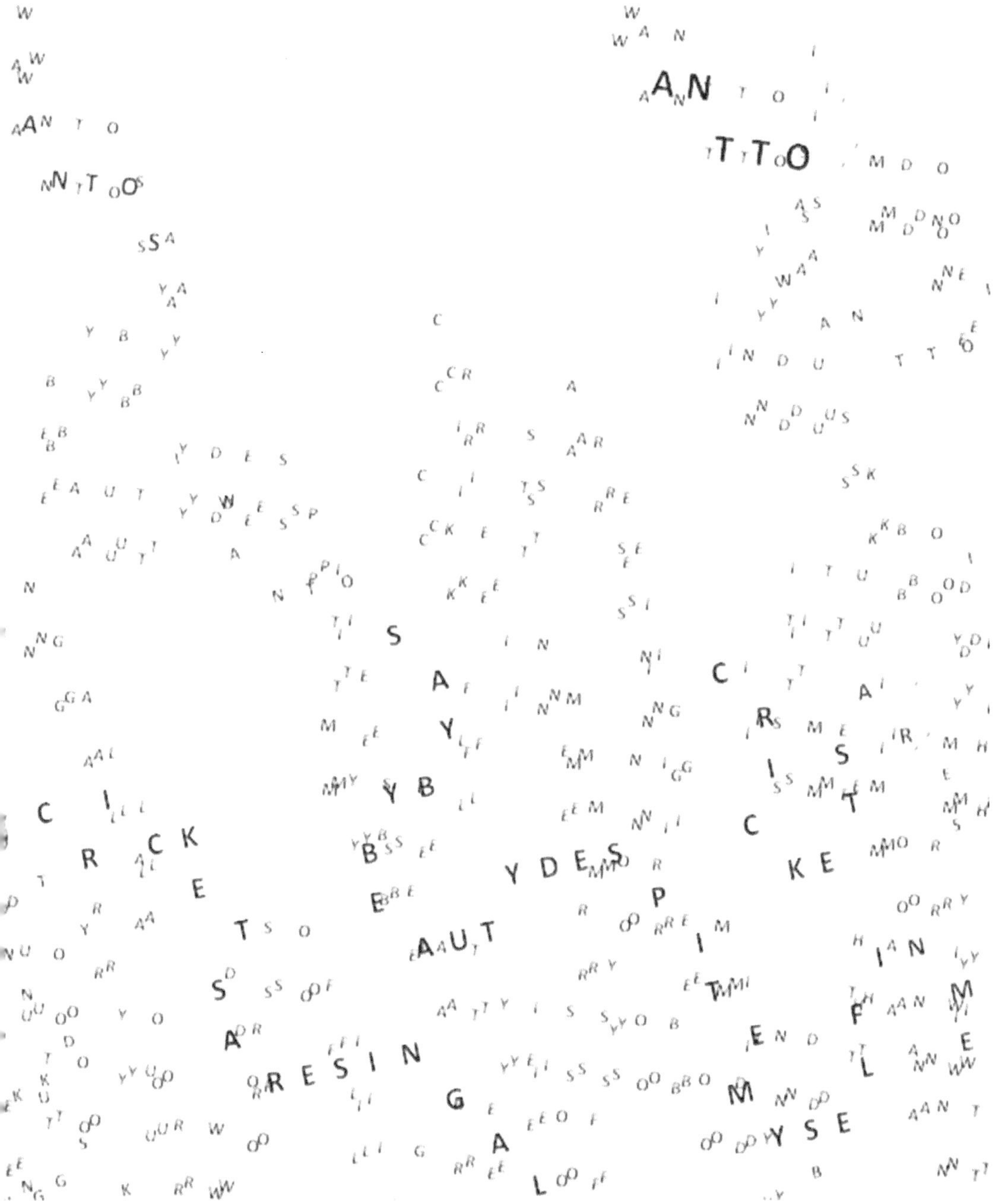

handled bloomed evening and our tongues

dragged among starlight

a shuttle of wind

a braided fog

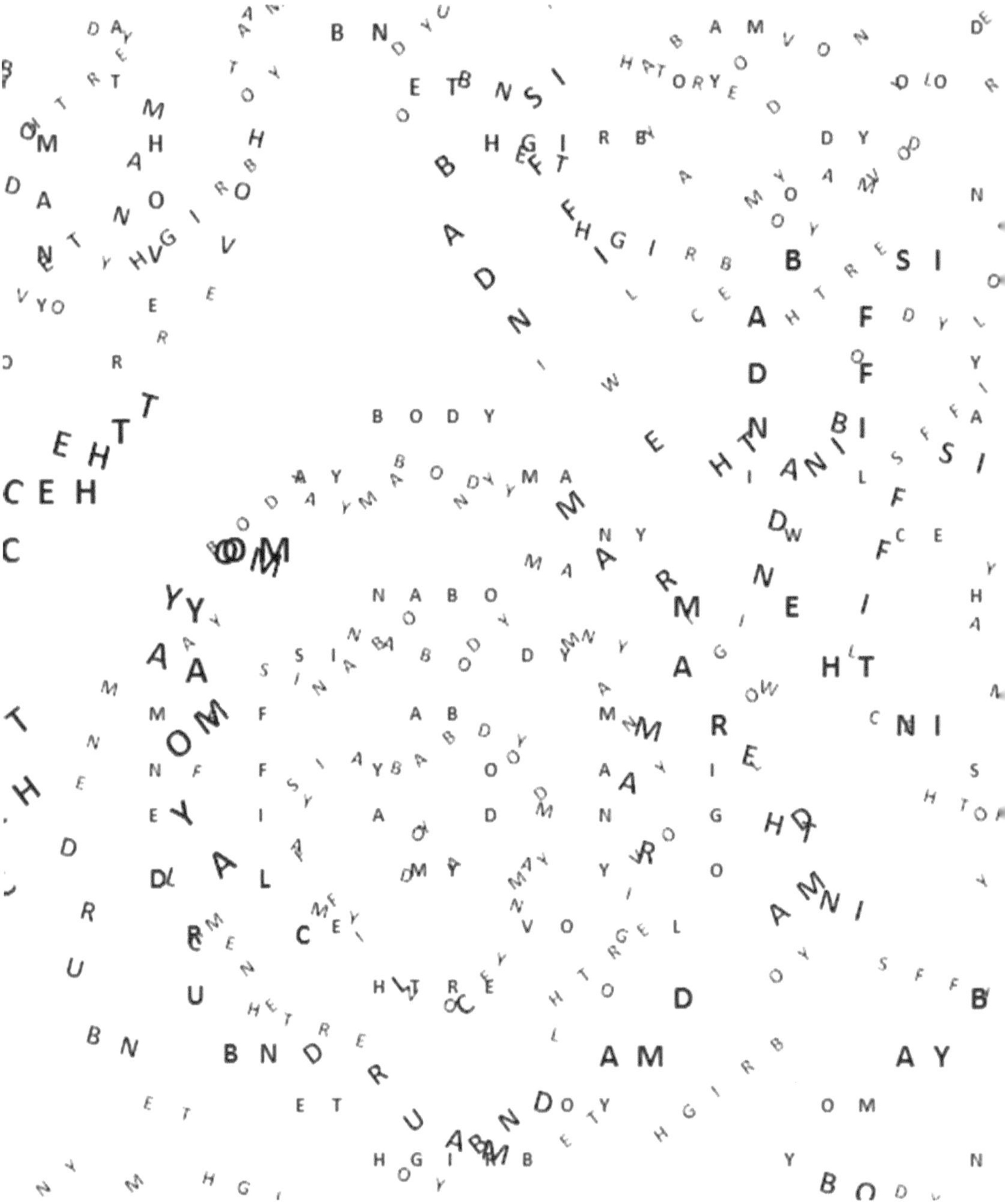

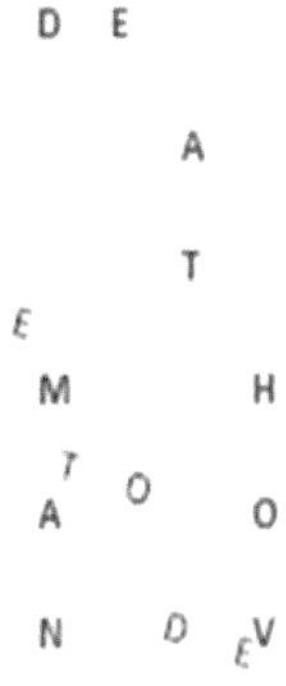

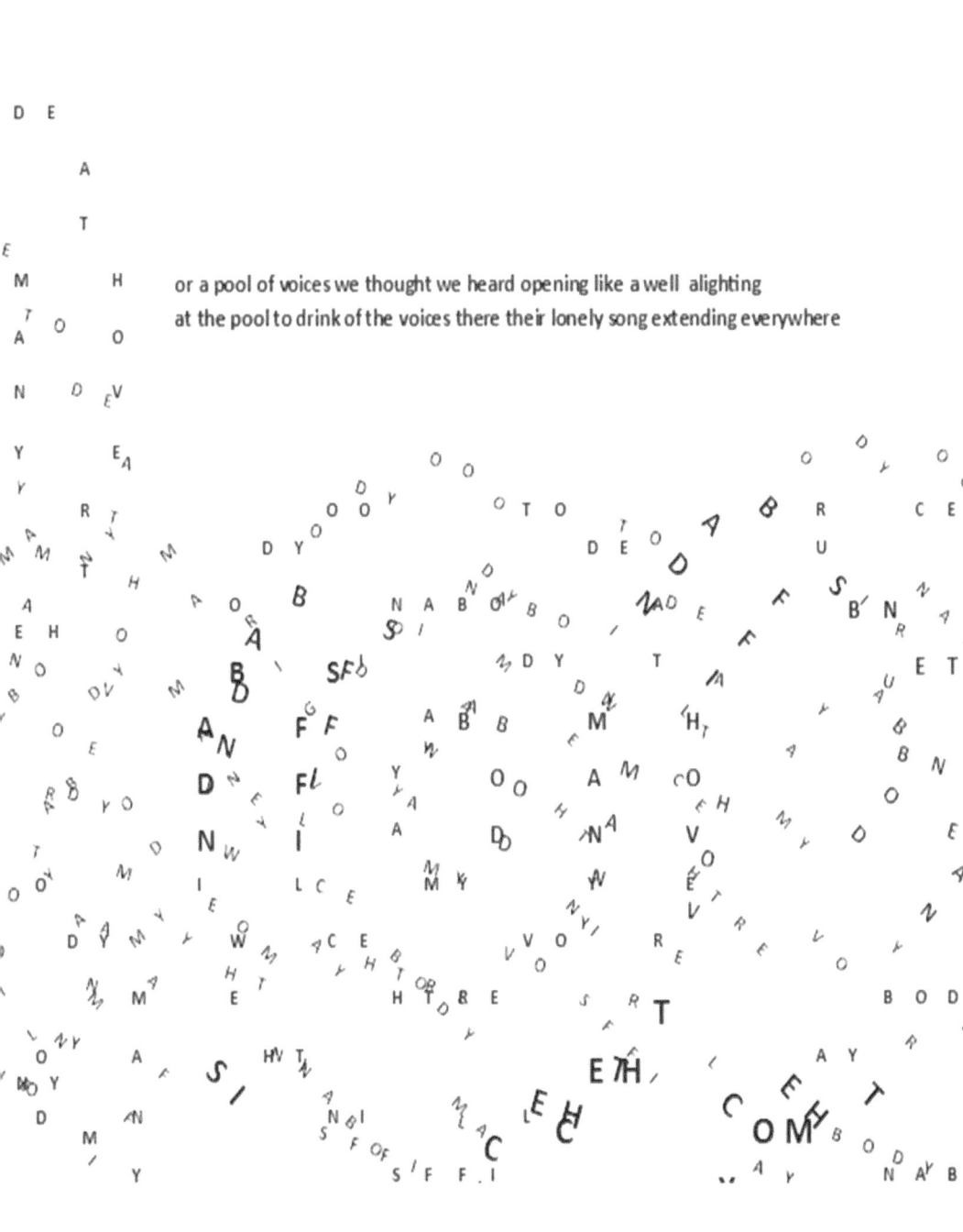

or a pool of voices we thought we heard opening like a well alighting
at the pool to drink of the voices there their lonely song extending everywhere

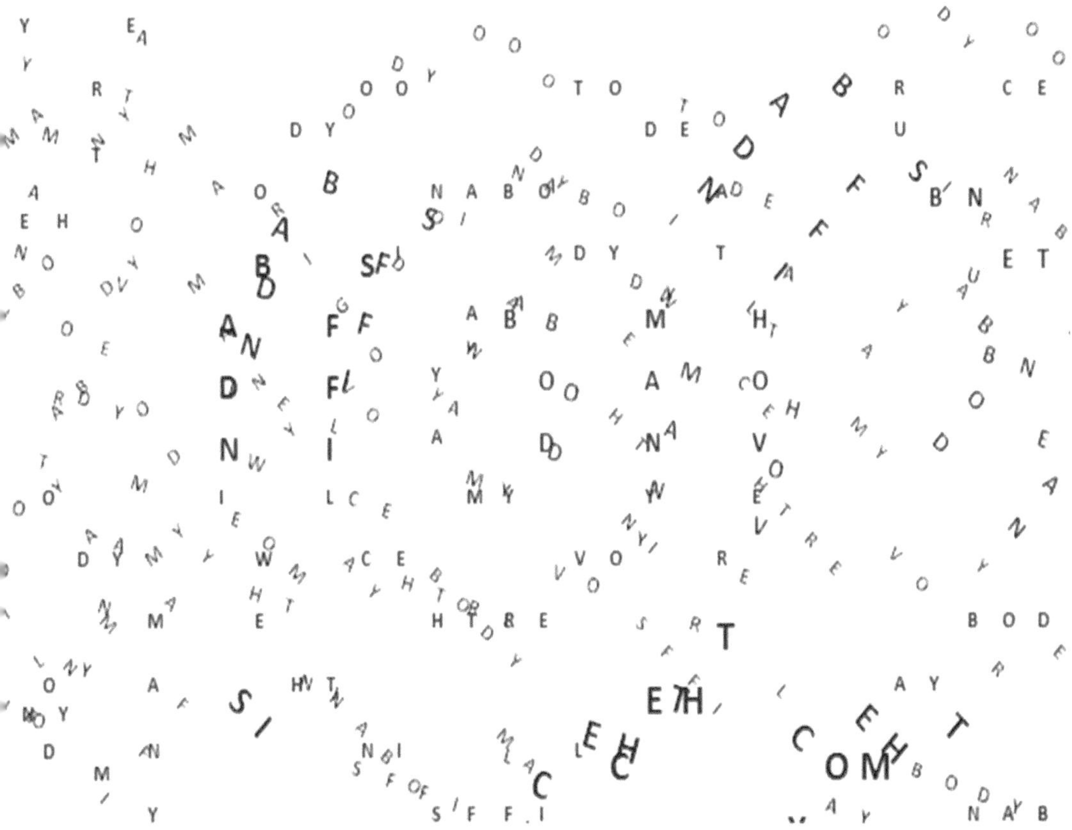

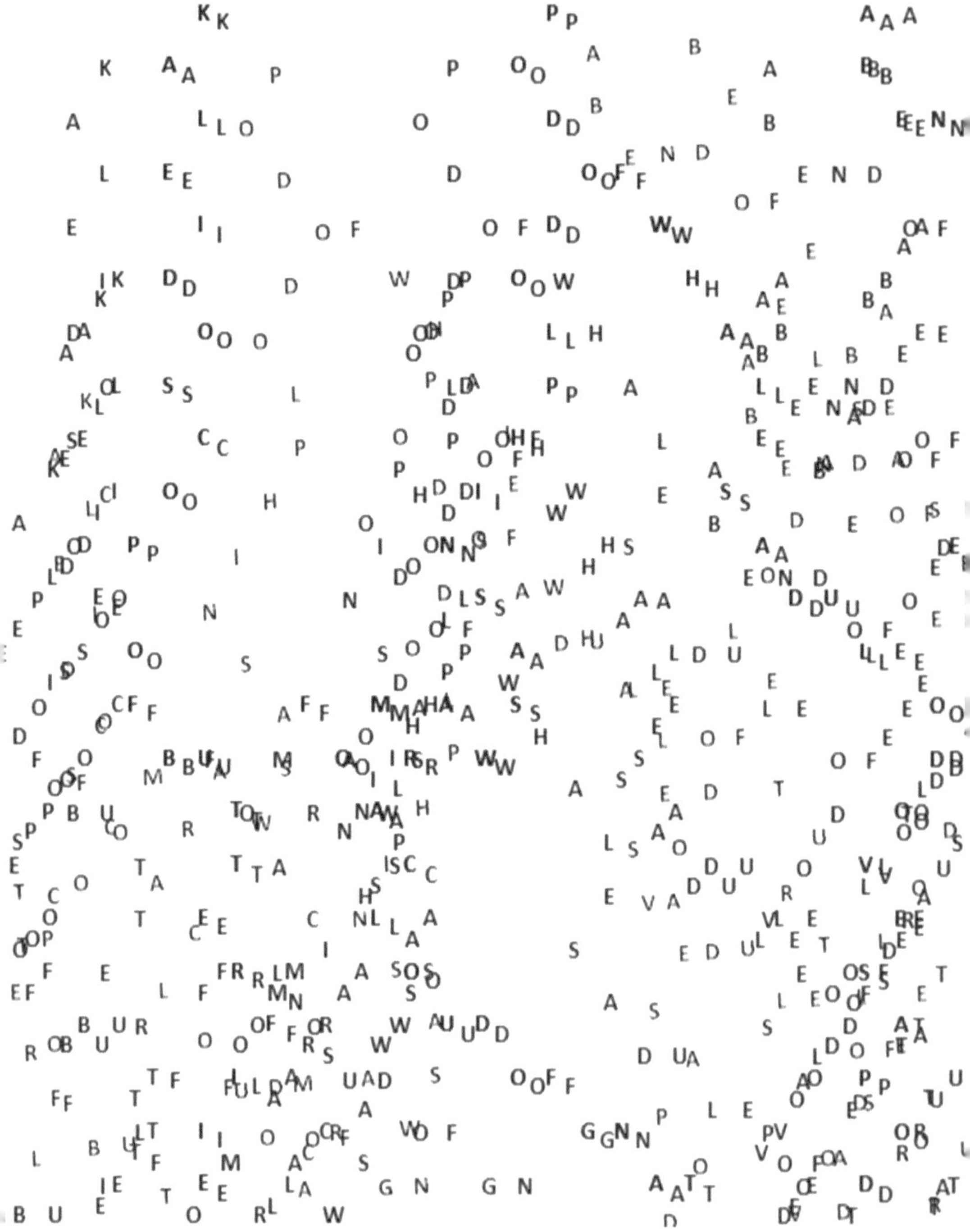

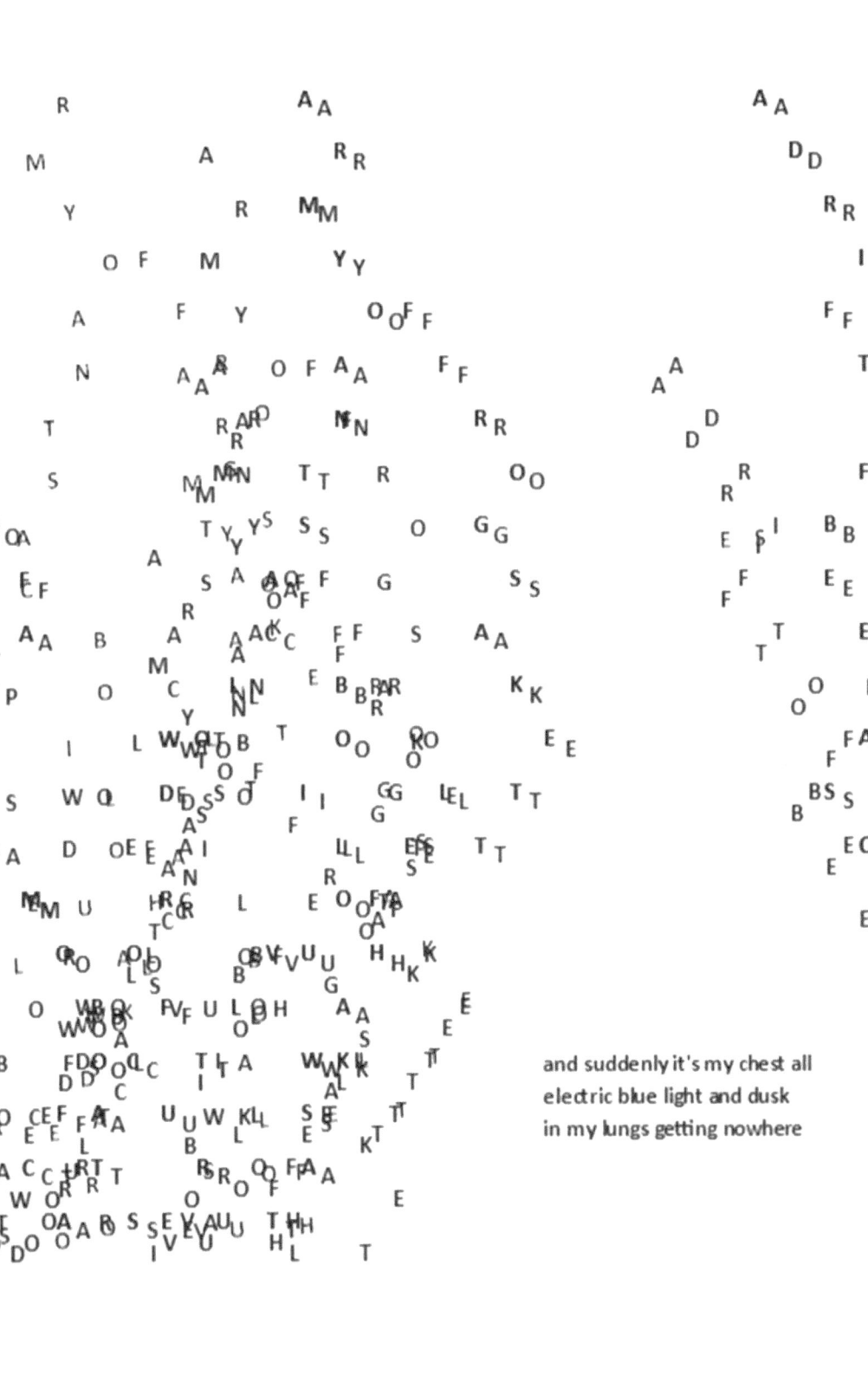

and suddenly it's my chest all
electric blue light and dusk
in my lungs getting nowhere

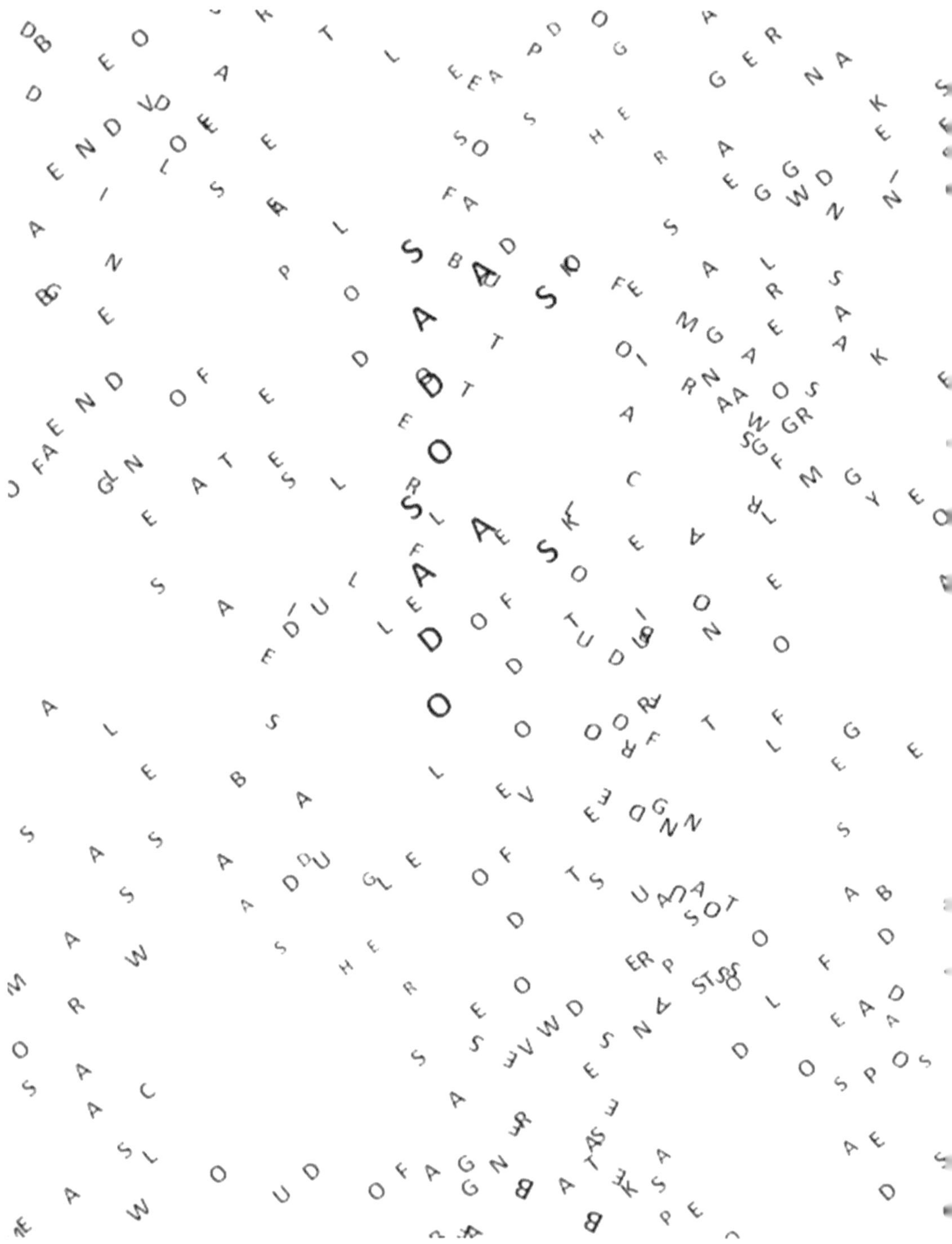

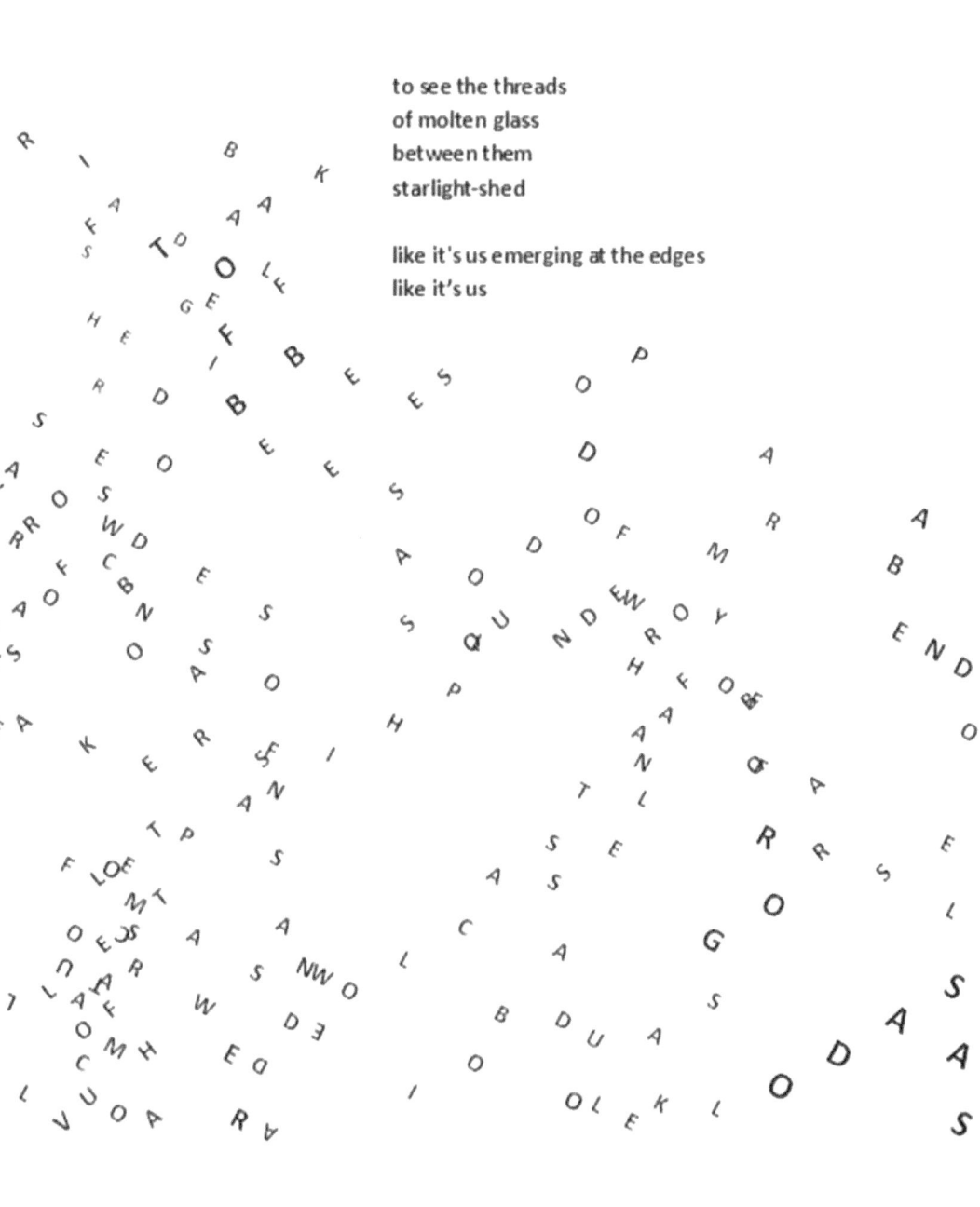

to see the threads
of molten glass
between them
starlight-shed

like it's us emerging at the edges
like it's us

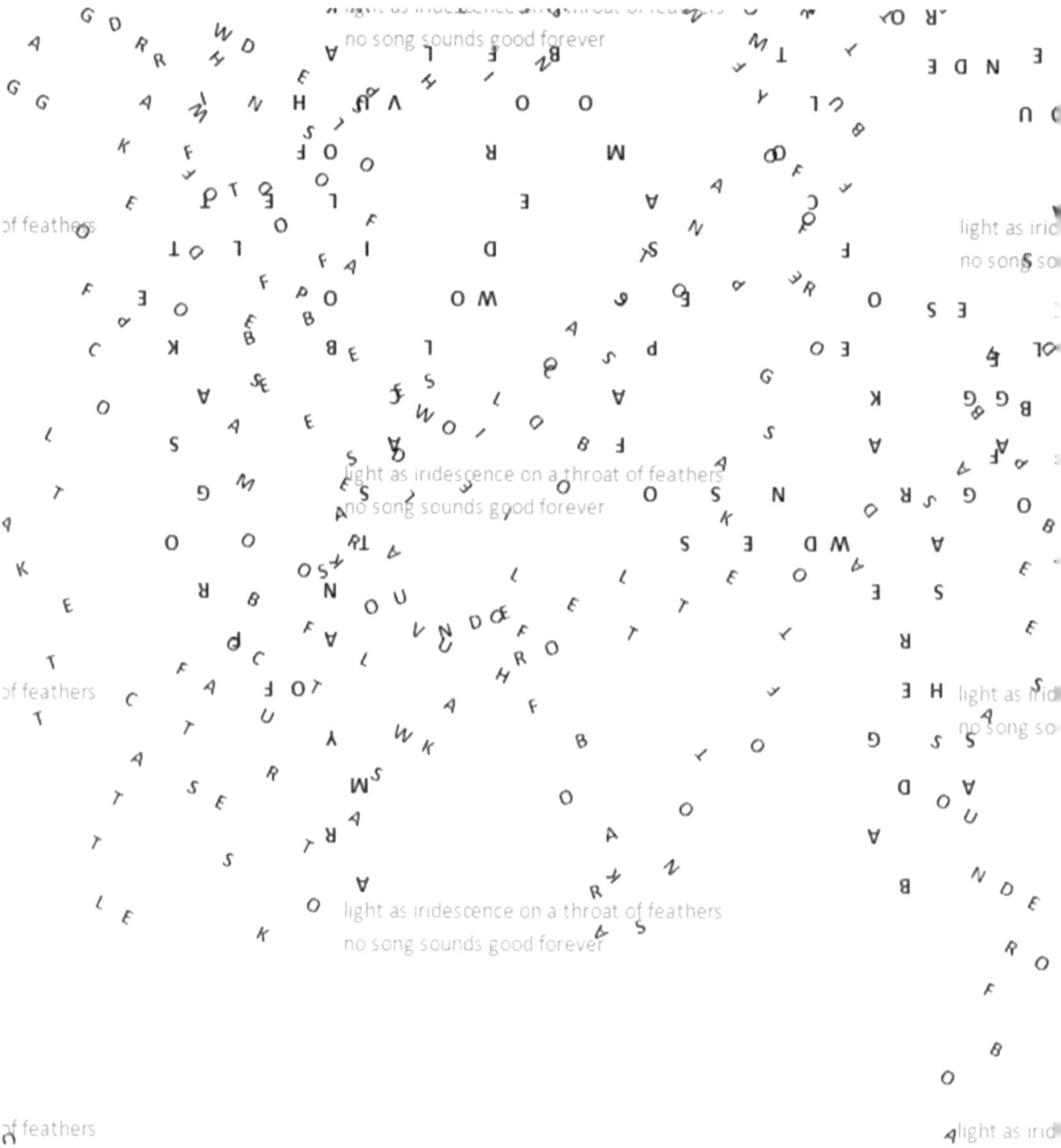
light as iridescence on a throat of feathers
no song sounds good forever
light as iridescence on a throat of feathers
no song sounds good forever
light as iridescence on a throat of feathers
no song sounds good forever

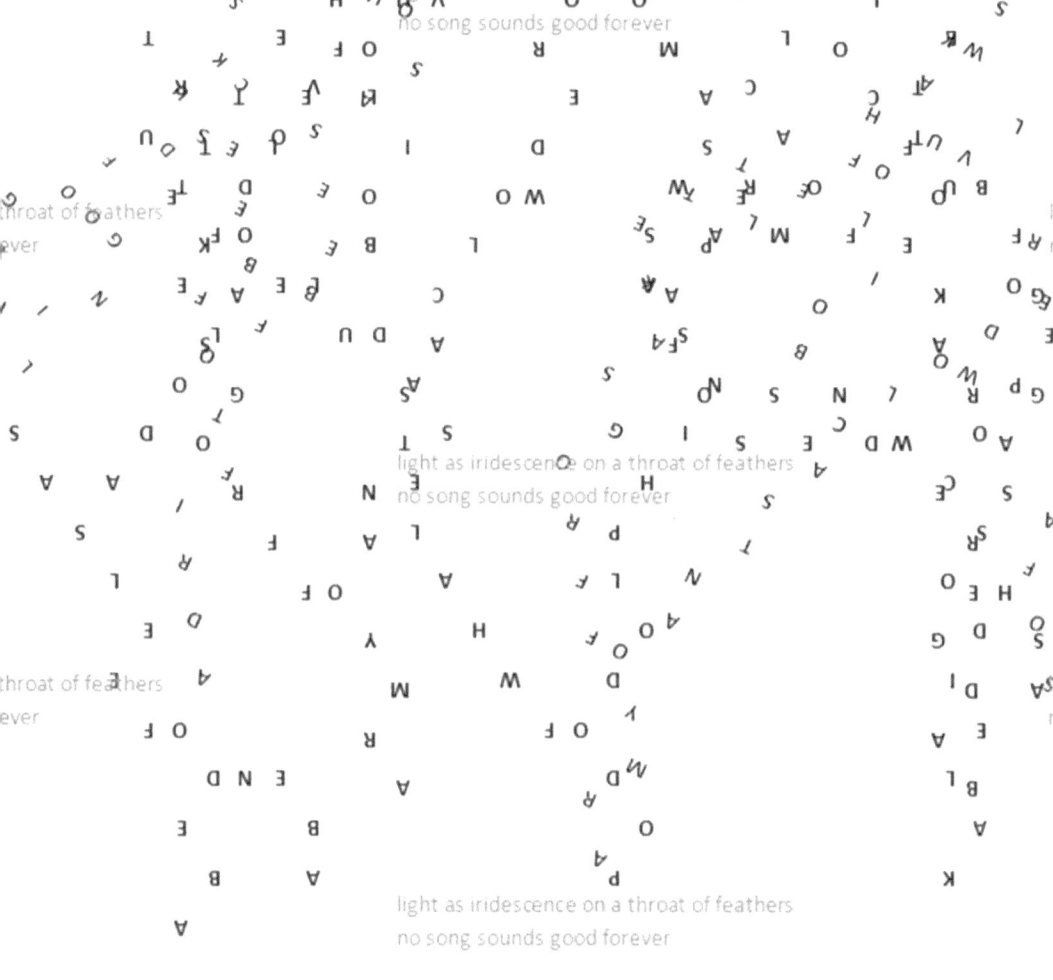

no song sounds good forever

throat of feathers
ever

light as iridescence on a throat of feathers
no song sounds good forever

throat of feathers
ever

light as iridescence on a throat of feathers
no song sounds good forever

throat of feathers

spool

I.

bandages
of snow
battered
blanket
pummeled
sheet
undertow
of oblit-
erating
white
indis-
crimin-
ate drift
stiff
stuff
flooded
crystal
gloom
come to
their single
note writ-
shredded
on waves
of vorti-
cal confetti

II.

one mi-
nute mo-
ment be-
(there)for(e)
I must
dally into
another
show-
ered shoe
shaved eye
combed
breath
and neck-
tie lolling
like a
tongue
despair-
ing thirst
I should-
er one mo-
re mi-
nute mo-
ment of s-
unlight on-
e more mi-
nuet of
sun be-
(there)for-
(e) this

III.

gravity waves
words make
space sponge-
bent to a figure
of accreted
hands forlorn
behind glass
case centur-
ies after you
called it speech-
growth, but
manageable
only as atoms
flailing goodbye

IIII.

hair wept
its curve
of pro-
teins and
it may have
been a will-
ow tree
in wat-
er's gently
aping cries
but some-
thing pools
to watch
you take
your feet
says I've
enough
of human-
ness shit
and sighs
to put
a mouth
into your
head then
bolts irre-
vocably
into the
extern-
ality of
its leaves

IIIII.

name-
less
wa-
ves
of
light
on
thi-
gh's
na-
me-
less
text-
ure
I am
bur-
ied a-
live
in the
bur-
den
of em-
bodi-
ment

moonlight triptych

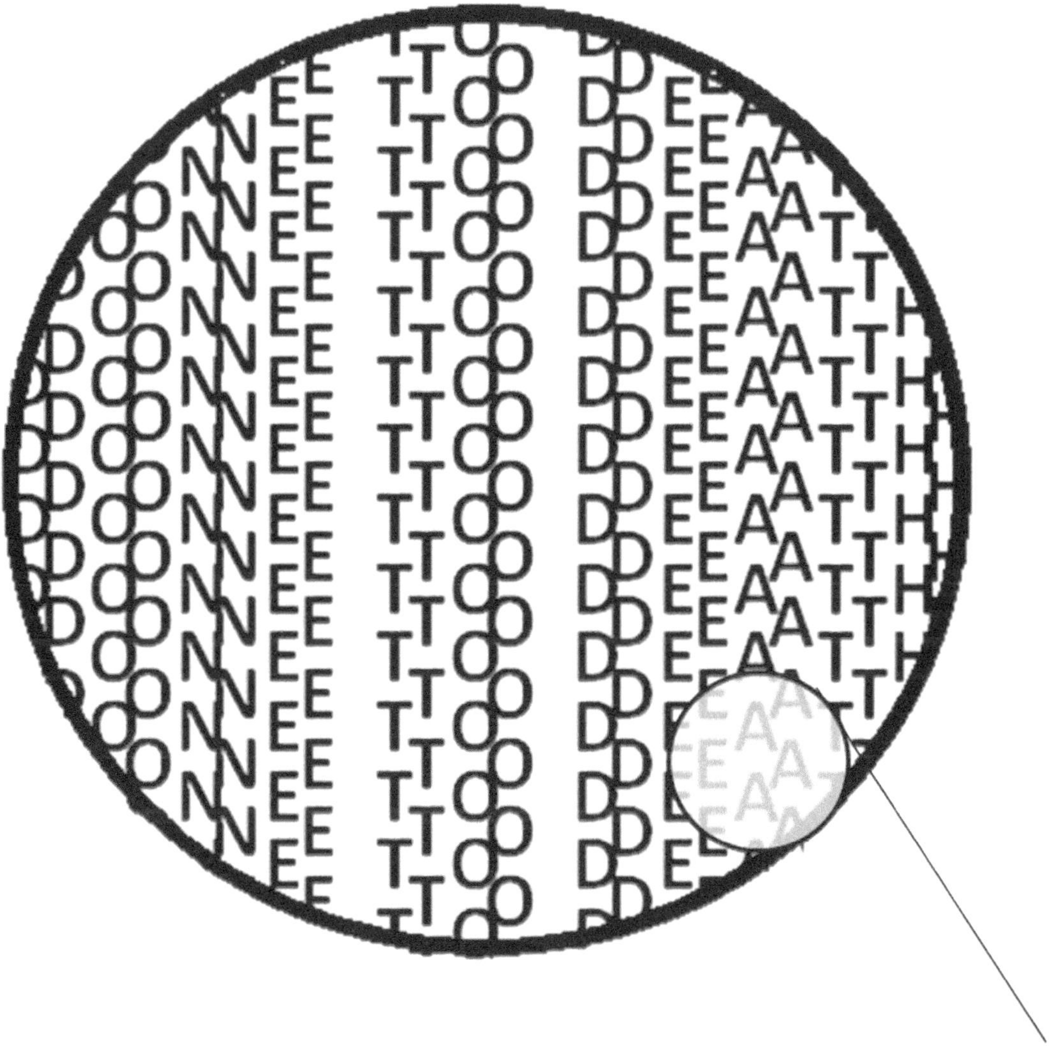

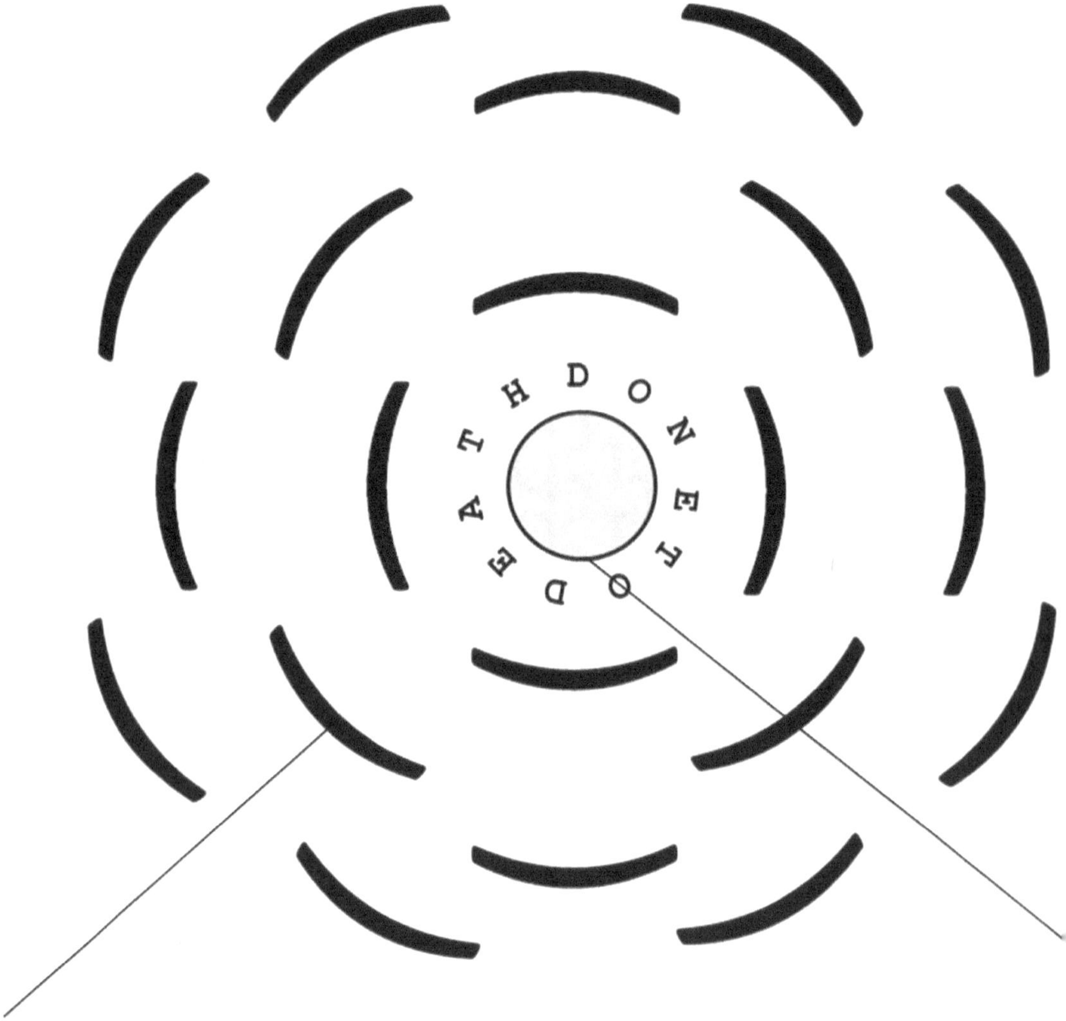
DEATH DONE TO

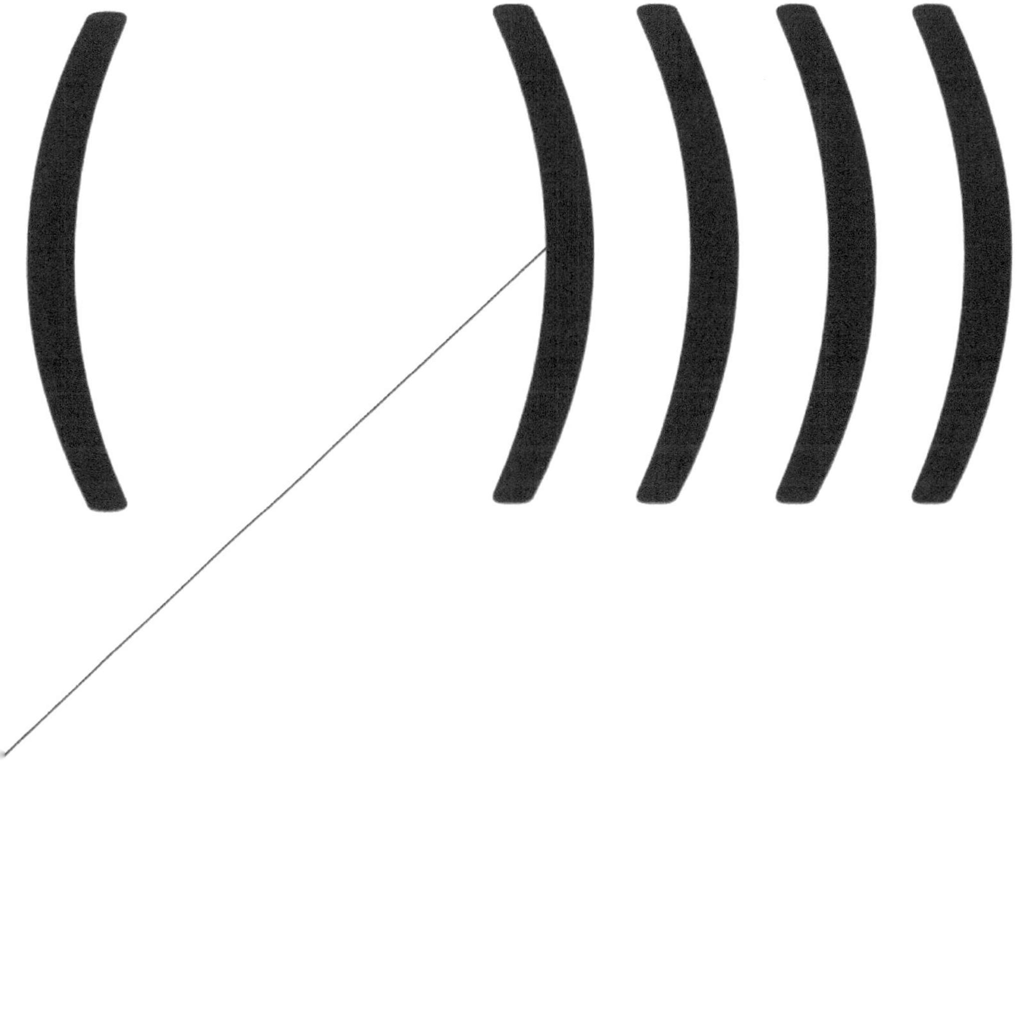

Acknowledgements

The author would like to thank the editors of the following journals where some of the poems in this collection first appeared: *E·ratio, Moss Trill, Otoliths, Pith,* and *Pot Luck*. The author would also like to thank Simulacrum Press for publishing the chapbook *Waterlight*.

About the Author

Andrew Brenza is an American experimental poet and librarian. His recent chapbooks include Poems in C (Viktlösheten Press), Bitter Almonds & Mown Grass (Shirt Pocket Press), Waterlight (Simulacrum Press), and Excerpt from Alphabeticon (No Press). His full-length collections of visual poetry include Gossamer Lid (Trembling Pillow Press), Automatic Souls (Timglaset Editions), Album, in Concrete (Alien Buddha Press) and Alphabeticon & Other Poems (RedFoxPress).

About the Press

Unsolicited Press is a small press in Portland, Oregon. The team publishes outstanding poetry, fiction, and creative nonfiction. Unsolicited Press is proud to have produced award-winning works from authors including John W. Bateman, Suzanne S. Rancourt, and Adrian Ernesto Cepeda.

Find the press on Twitter and Instagram.

Learn more at unsolicitedpress.com.

www.ingramcontent.com/pod-product-compliance
Lightning Source LLC
Chambersburg PA
CBHW030132100526
44591CB00009B/625
9781950730612